Treasured Island

Madagascar

In *Treasured Island* Unknown Fields travels through Madagascar to catalogue the push and pull of economy and ecology and meet the illegal traders of the world's luxury brands. Through interview fragments and investigative photography we unravel the black market supply chain that strings the precious gem stones from the wild west mining towns of Madagascar to the celebrity necklines and trembling newlywed fingers of the city.

In times past an anarchist community of pirates called Madagascar home. It was an island beyond the law and off the map, a place of rogues, booty and bounties. These were outlaws moored on a marooned ecosystem. Set adrift 88 million years ago, the island is a castaway in the Indian Ocean, inhabited by a band of ecological stowaways. In this splendid isolation it has evolved into an unparalleled wonderland of the weird and unique, diverse and unbelievable. A political coup in 2009 left the country adrift once more — isolated from the international community, deprived of foreign aid and conservation funding. One of the planet's most precious ecological treasures is home to one of its poorest nations and it raises difficult and complex questions about the relationship between necessity and luxury. In the shadows of the world's desires we uncover some of the complex value negotiations that play out across this unique island where village farms are measured against habitat and bodies are quantified as a mechanical resource. We witness a territory that is equally wondrous and scarred, a choreography of global resource extraction that dances in the heart of the most unique ecosystem on the planet.

Rare tortoises leave in rucksacks, forests are carved into million dollar rosewood beds to be sold in China and precious stones are shovelled from the earth and smuggled onto the screen in popstar bling. As the beat drops and the stage lights strobe they flash their jewelled gold teeth for the camera in a flurry of choreographed dance moves. A world away, in a hole in the ground in the wild west mining town of Ilakaka, Madagascar, another choreography of bodies move in rhythm, to dig dirt by hand out of the bottom of a precious gem mine. Hidden amidst political uncertainty, the island's fragile and unique ecology is being illegally exported, boat by boat, stone by stone.

Three hunned thou, five hunned thou

A million, let's have a money shower

51°44'N
51°5.79"W

Gold all up in my grill

Rollin' in MPVs, every week we made forty Gs

Cash rules

Dollar, dollar bill y'all

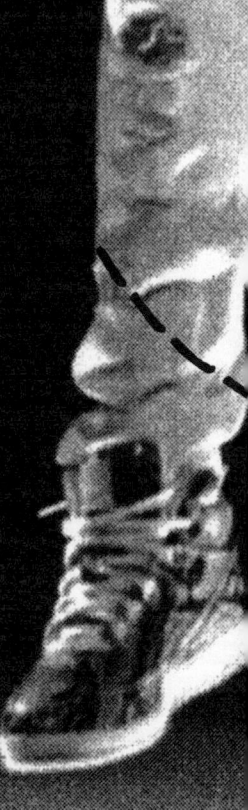

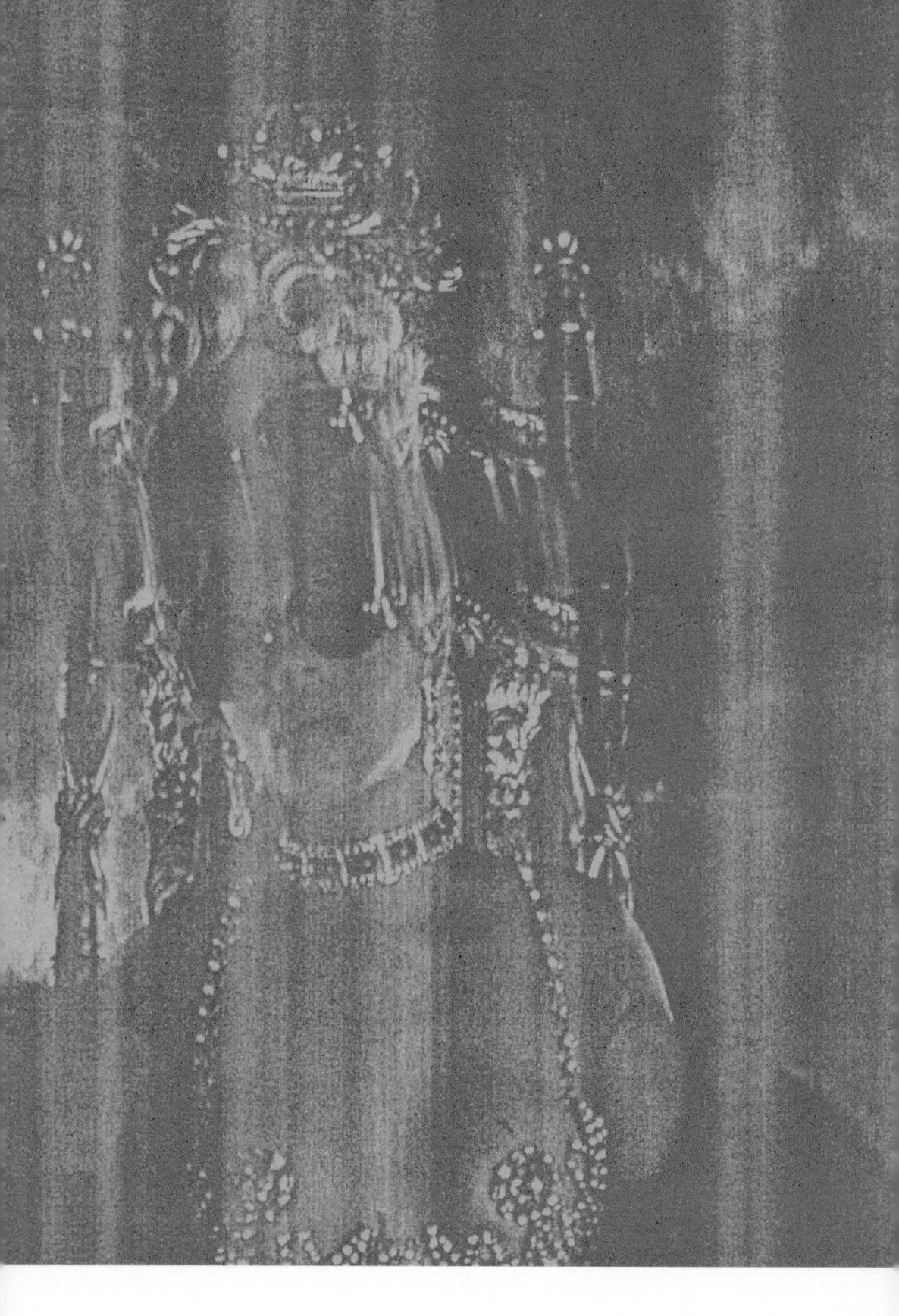

Thirty per cent of the world's sapphires are pulled out of the ground by the human conveyor belts of one small town in Madagascar's gem fields. For such a remote island it contains an extraordinary amount of high-value resources. Precious gems were deposited here by an ancient river that once flowed across Africa before a tectonic shift ripped it from the mainland to form the island of Madagascar. The stones collected in a pocket along the twists and turns of the riverbed, resting patiently, beneath 20m of sand and the future boom town of Ilakaka.

    We sit down and talk with Mark Nouvera, a daunting man and mine boss, one of the major players in present day Ilakaka. One of the few Europeans in town, he moved here 18 years ago, chasing the stones, hunting his fortune. He is the anonymous face reflected in every piece of jewellery you own.

to
try and
find the
river
again

Each worker gets $2 a day to work in the mines

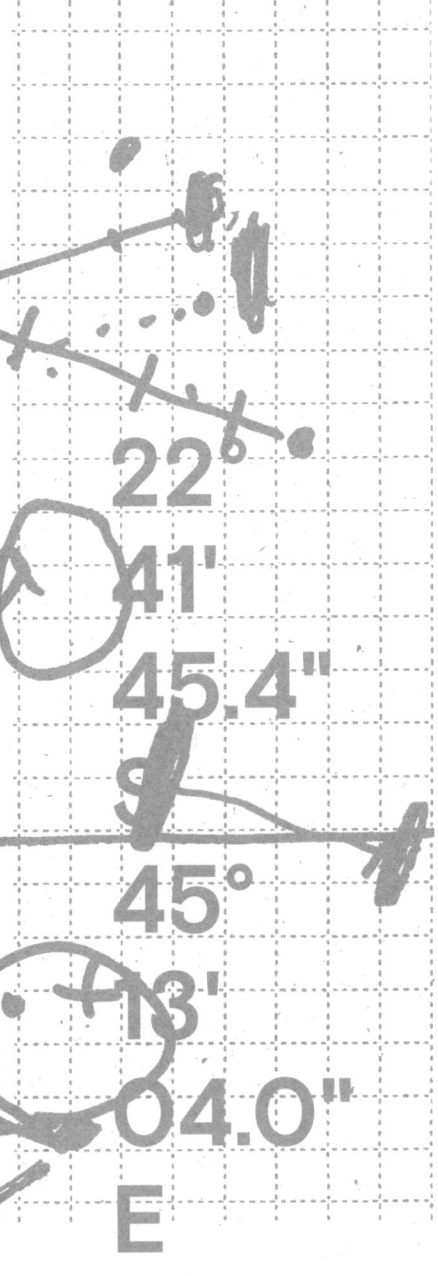

I finance the pit. Here in Ilikaka the land is free, all you need to mine is a local arrangement with the chiefs and elders. There is no government here. There is nothing. There are thousands of people here but it is the most lonely place in Madagascar.

In 1999 he drove into Ilakaka, to live in a tent and watch the place explode. When he first arrived there was only one building here and now the landscape is overrun with almost 100,000 miners. There is only one road in or out and it is lined with gem shops and sweaty men, with guns on their hip.

This is a landscape produced from unregulated desires. If you want to mine with machines you need a formal contract and money for fuel and maintenance.

I like stone better than humans, and I like stone better than money.
To dig with people you don't need anything, just a bag of rice.
When you find the good dirt you start with a small hole just big enough for a body to fit in. If you continue to get good dirt you make it bigger.

and 50g of rice

1m³ of earth =

1 gram of gemstone

Here it is cheaper to pay workers in rice than it is to buy and maintain mechanical mining equipment. The 20 men of his 'Swiss Bank' mine shovel dirt in perfect synchronisation, each paid with 50g of rice, their bodies repurposed as machines.

We trace their movements in space in the manner of Frank Gilbreth's early photography studies. He was mapping the choreographies of the production line, looking to optimise every movement, constrain every motion with the elegance of a tuned engine. The digger is a robot, just one component in the gemstone conveyor belt.

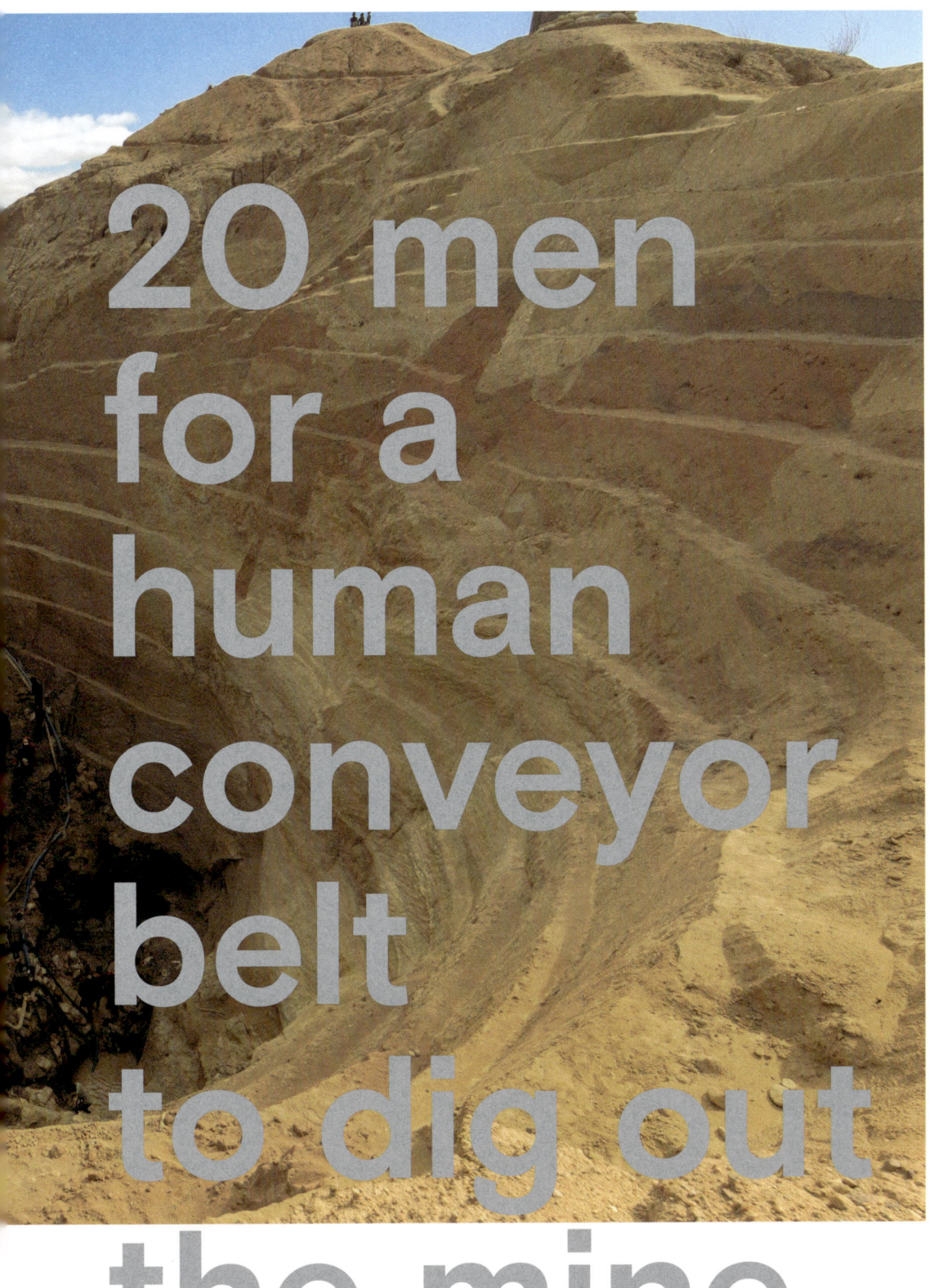

20 men for a human conveyor belt to dig out the mine

We are allowed to go and meet one of the diggers working out in the fields. It is an alien landscape where each step can plunge you 30m down a hole of empty promise.

This is my hole, I started digging four years ago. Every hole here was made by our hands.

If they catch people stealing then they will drop them down a hole with no rope.

If you are lucky you find a good sapphire and you have a good life. With no luck you die, or you grow old digging holes.

When we find a stone we go all together to the Sri Lankan's to sell it and split the money. We don't know what happens to them or the stones. We don't know how much money they sell them for, the money never comes back to us. Malagasy people don't have any possibility to sell to people outside. We miss out on everything.

2,880 shovels per day,

5.76 tonnes

per day

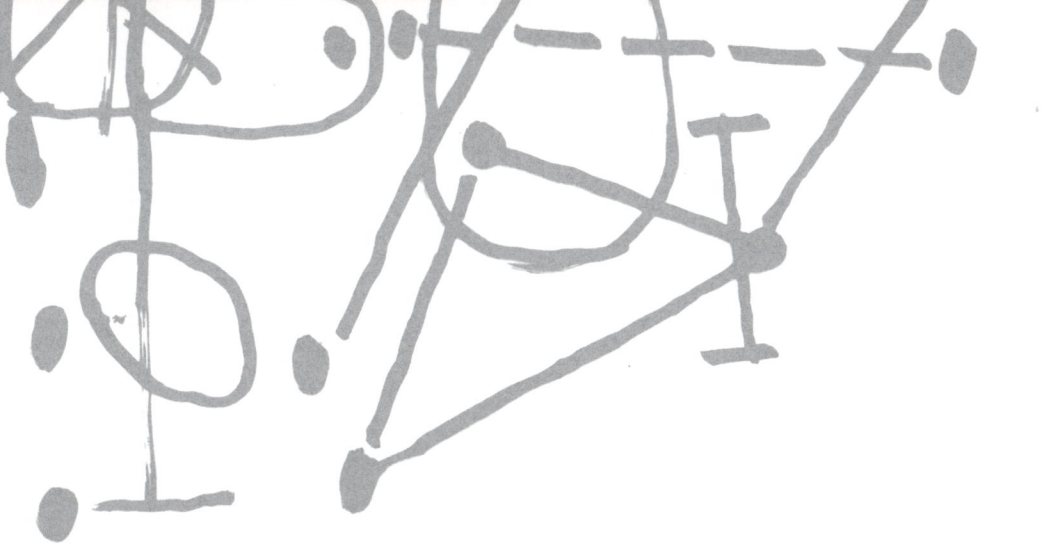

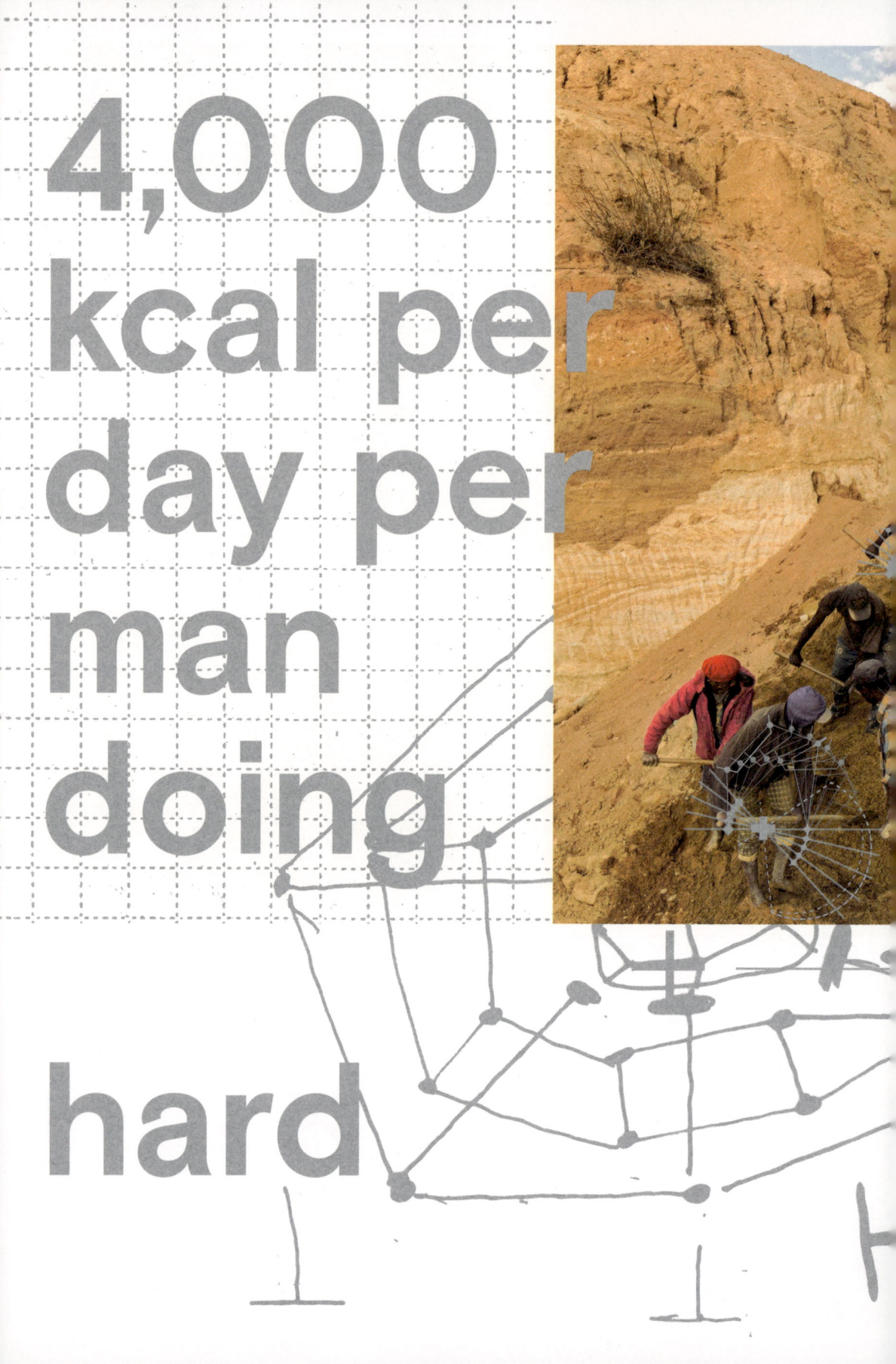

4,000 kcal per day per man doing

hard

Beside our host everyone else with money in this town is Sri Lankan. The cultural relationship to sapphires runs deep in Sri Lanka. Embedded within this tradition Sri Lankan sapphires sell at a much better price than Madagascan stones. If rough, unpolished stones can be smuggled out of the country and back to Sri Lanka they can be refined and sold on at an extraordinary markup.

It's called baby blue. Blue sapphire is sold for $1,000

a carat if it can be smuggled back into Sri Lanka

Ilakaka gem buyers are

90% Sri Lankan
9% Thai
1% European

At 6pm the single-street town comes alive as
miners return from the field for a treacherous
two-hour negotiation over the sale of the day's
pickings. They crowd around the tiny grilled
windows that line the street and watch as a
Sri Lankan inside sorts through their finds.
The street is washed with the focused light
of a hundred tiny gem torches shining through
stones looking for imperfections and inclusions,
anything to drop the price.

We find ways to send rough stones out of the country. If I find a good stone I fly back to Switzerland to get a certificate on which I can nominate the origin of the stone. I make much more money if I say I got it from Sri Lanka.

You buy a Malagasy stone in Sri Lanka under the Sri Lankan or Burmese name. It is easier to sell Ceylon Blue than Madagascar.

quotes 2,100kcal as a minimum daily intake

We are not a city,

we have no name, no mayor, no bank, no map

We imagine planes full of buyers, lifting off from this treasured island, their shoes and their jacket linings full of shimmering, deep blue jewels.

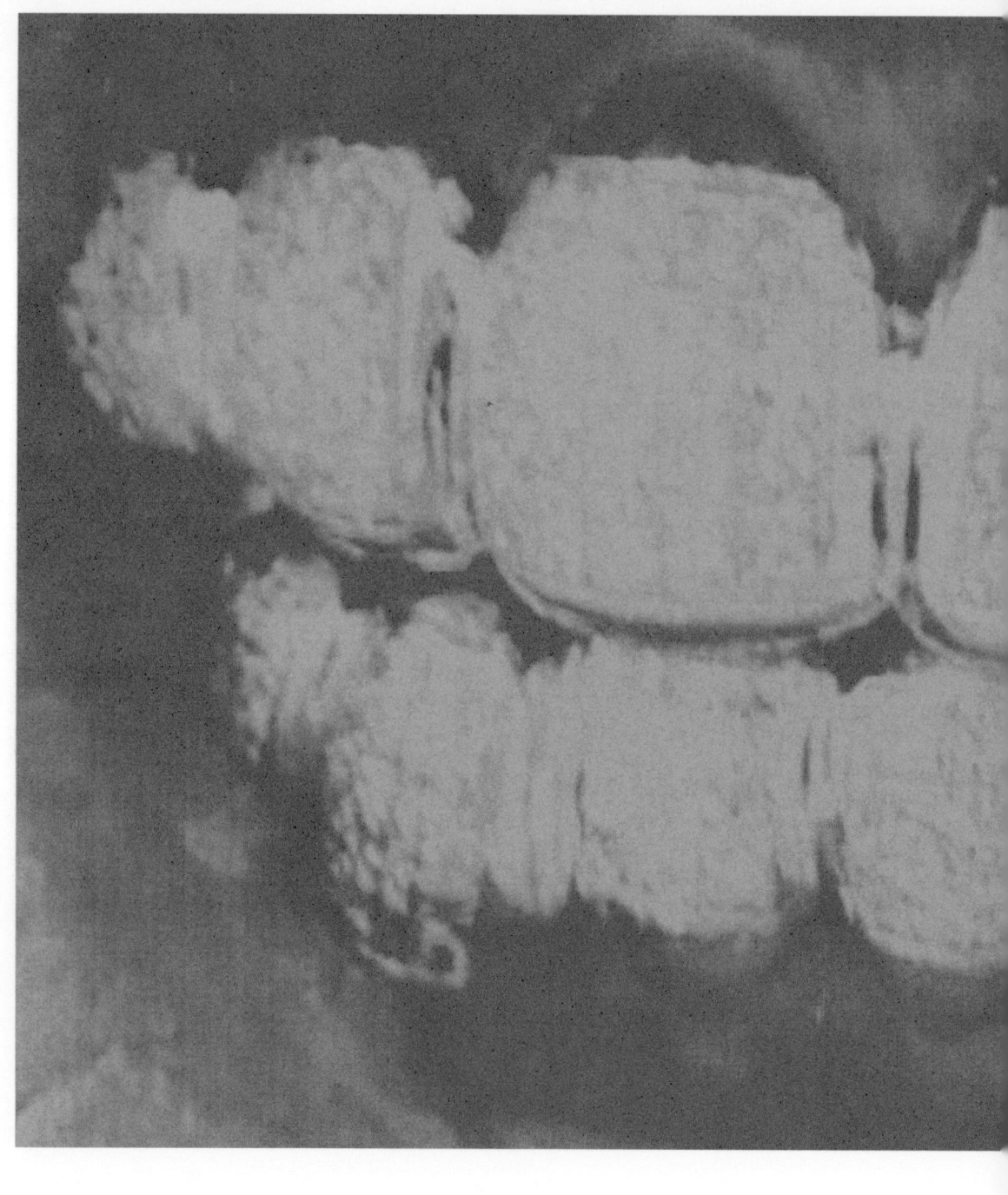

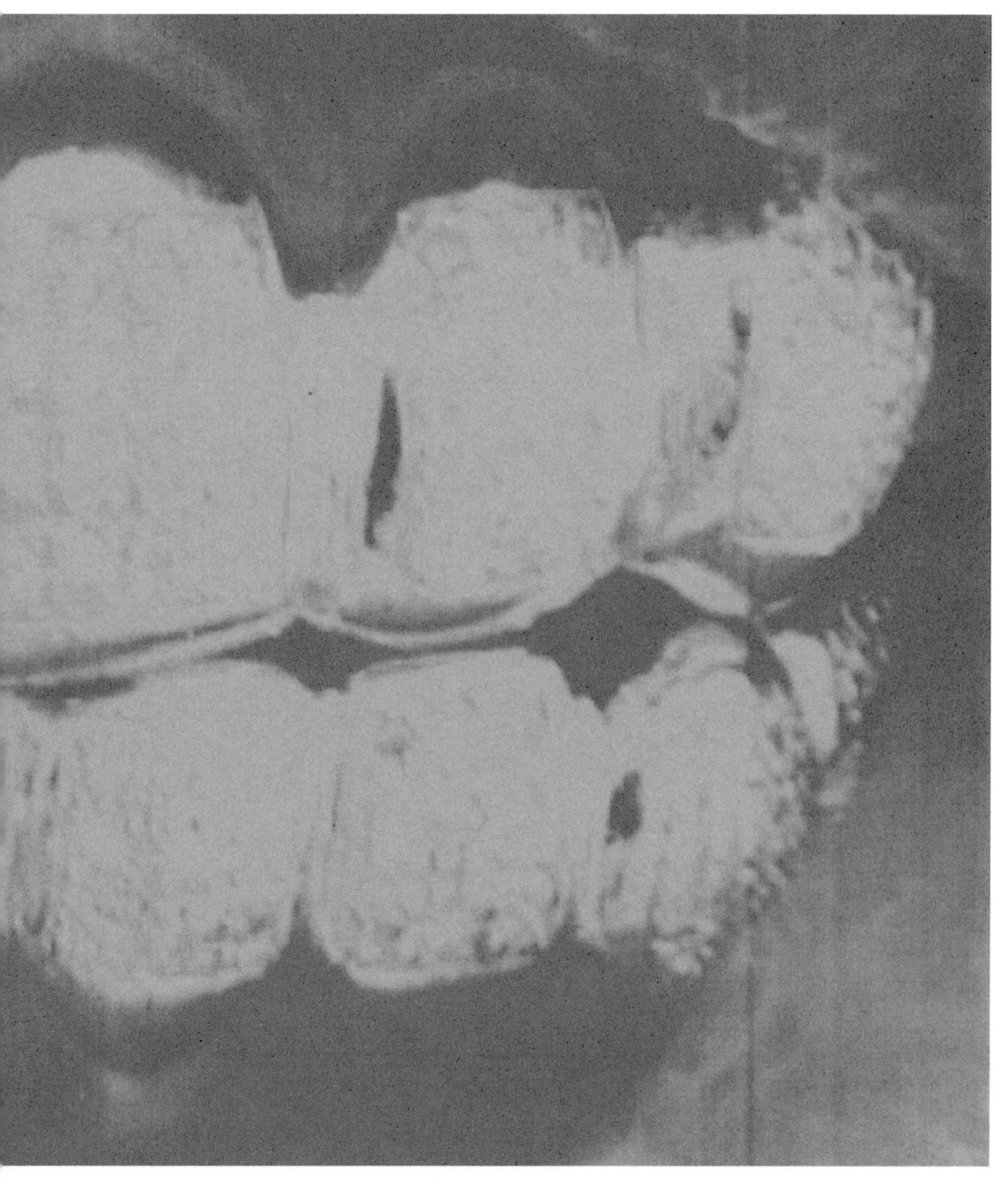

A hidden black market supply chain connects these two choreographies, from the lawless mine sites to the jewellery stores, hip hop music videos and celebrity red carpets across the ocean. Material production and cultural production have never been separate.

All Up in My Grill

Unknown Fields have used the amount of rice the human conveyor belt consumes in a day to manufacture a precious stone that embodies the systems through which these worlds are intimately and profoundly connected.

The red Madagascan rice grown endemically on this
treasured island is a staple food of the miners
and has been collected locally and shipped to
gem specialists for carbon analysis.

Unknown Fields have formed a synthetic stone

By subjecting the rice to extreme heat and pressure in the laboratory, Unknown Fields have formed a synthetic stone encoded with the sum of the human conveyor belt's labour.

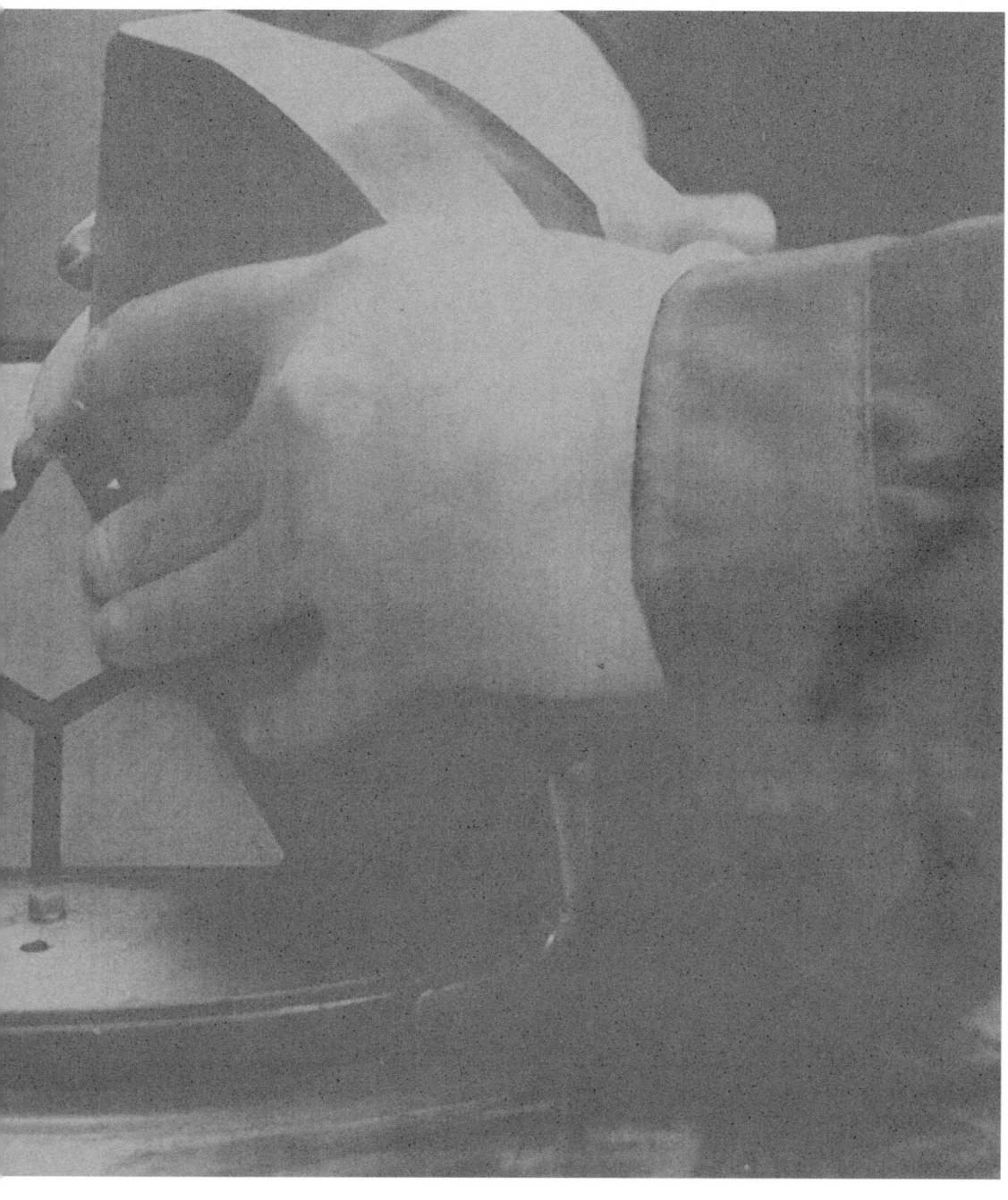

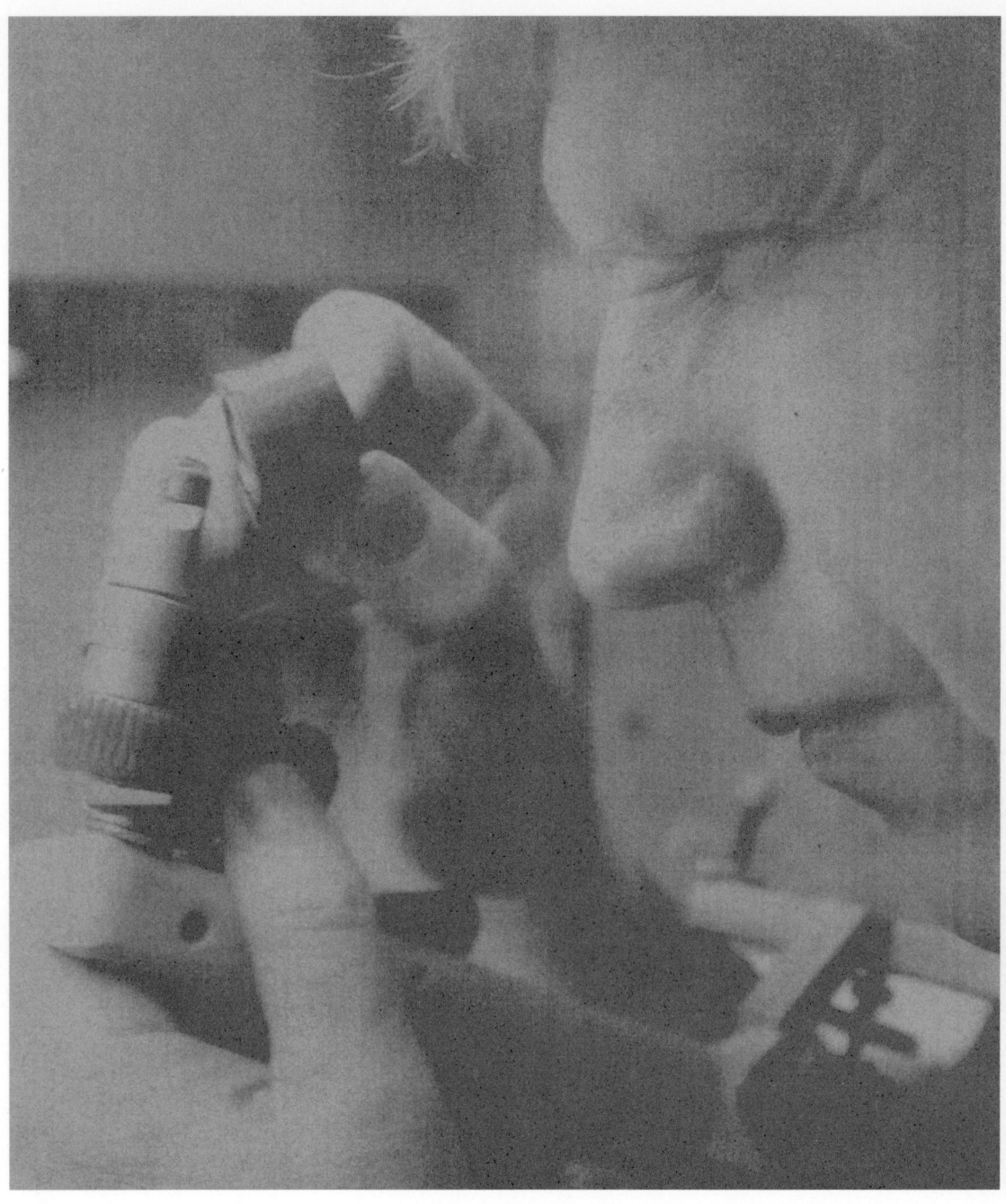

20 men shovelling

After manufacture, the gemstone has been set into a gold tooth, ready for that million-dollar smile and the outrageous lyric. From kilojoules, to carats, to the nightclub. In the glare of this cheeky gold grin we see the cost of luxury, of beauty, of a daily allowance of rice, of 20 men shovelling at the bottom of a hole.

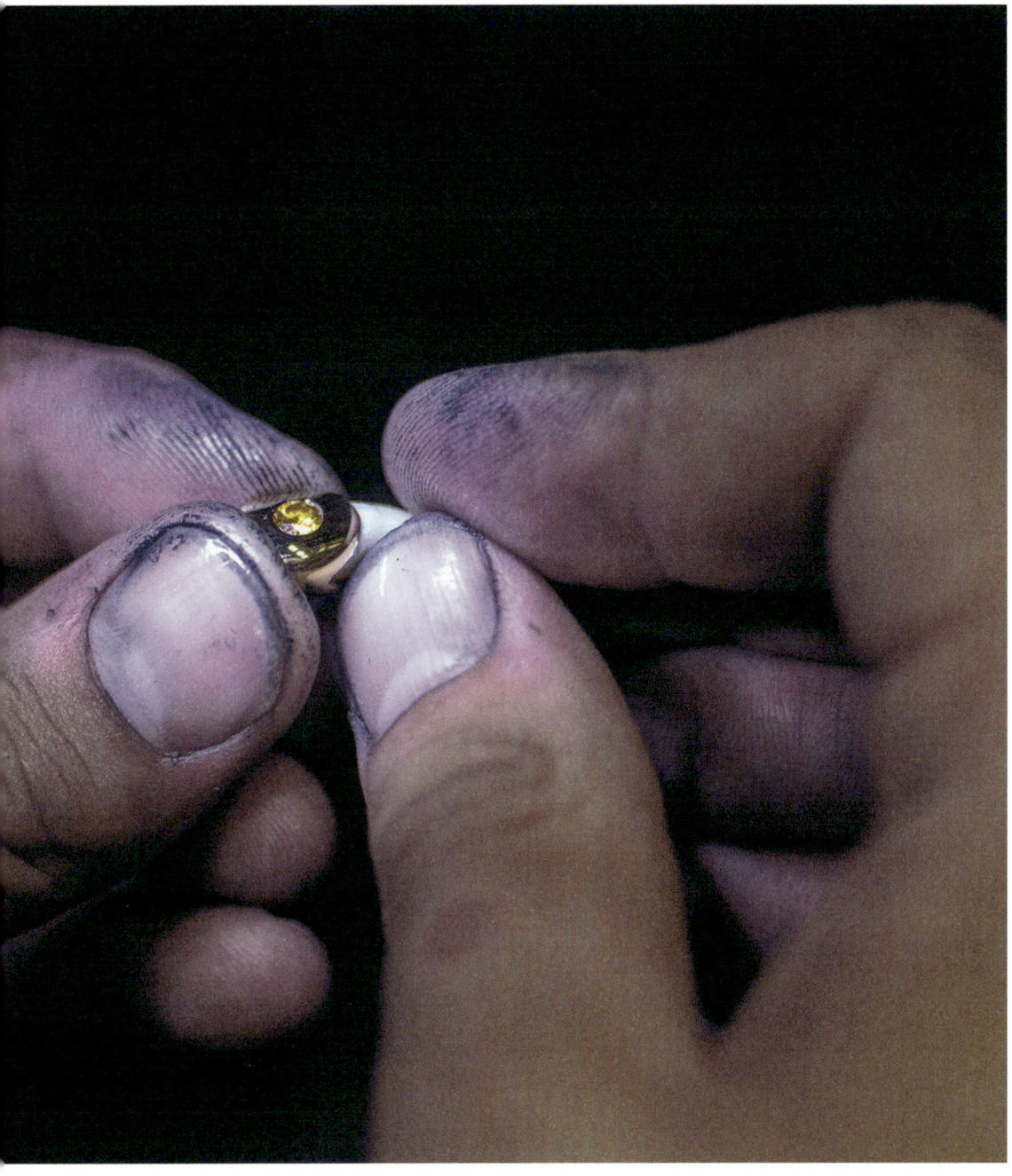

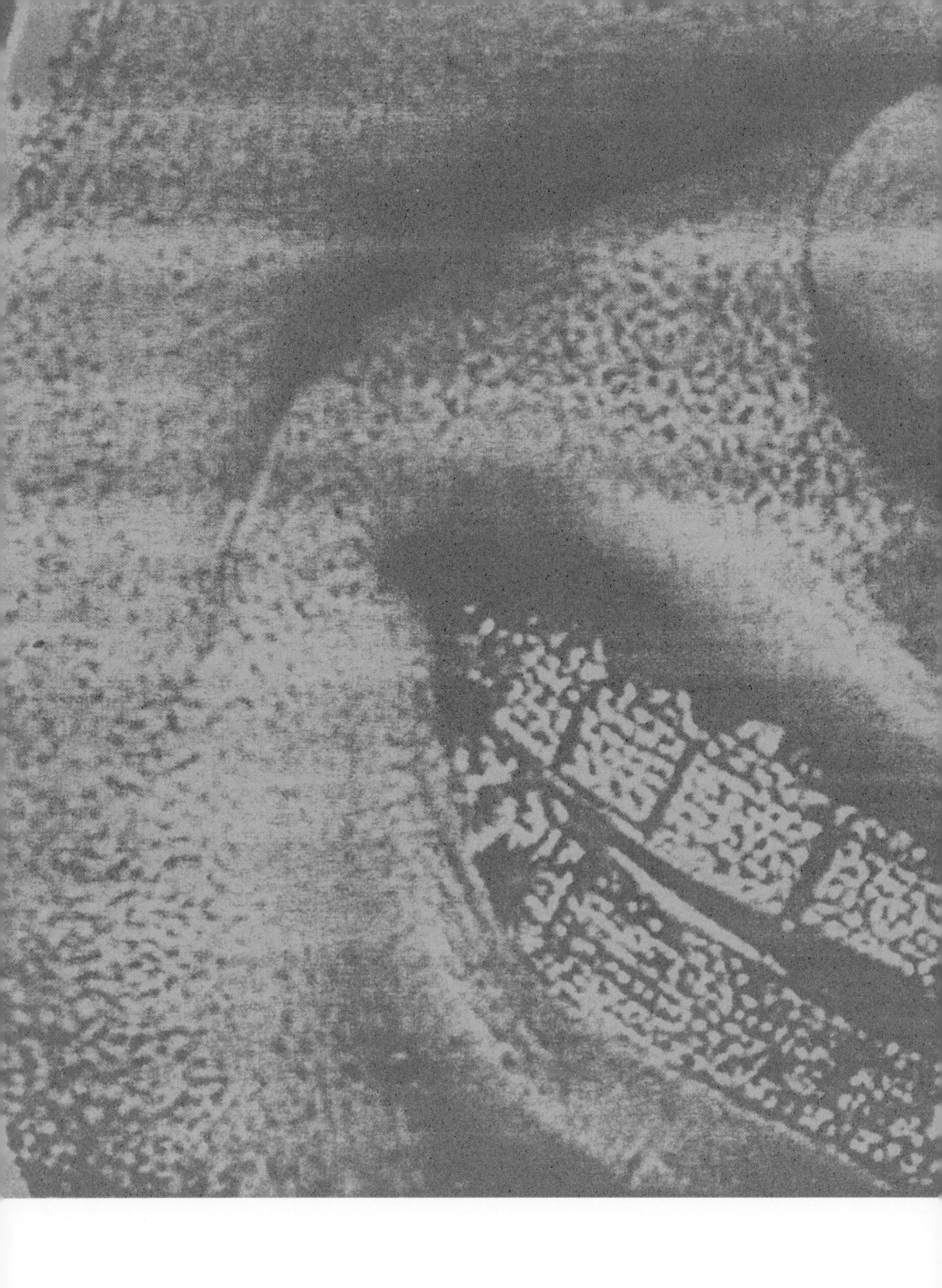

It glistens in the light and, mirrored in the facets of the rice diamond, we see ourselves.

Treasured Island by Unknown Fields

Design: Neasden Control Centre & City Edition Studio
Illustration: Neasden Control Centre

Printed in Italy by Musumeci S.p.a.
ISBN 978-1-907896-87-3

© 2016 Architectural Association and the Author

No part of this book may be reproduced in any manner whatsoever without written permission from the publisher, except in the context of reviews

For a catalogue of AA Publications visit aaschool.ac.uk/publications or email publications@aaschool.ac.uk

AA Publications
36 Bedford Square
London
WC1B 3ES
t + 44 (0)20 7887 4021
f + 44 (0)20 7414 0783